Cyber security and the world

Exposing cyber crime and solutions

Joel pearson

DEDICATION

This book is dedicated to all and sundry because the issue of cyber security affects everyone in all ways.

CONTENTS

ACKNOWLEDGMENTS

INTRODUCTION

The use of technologies, procedures, and policies to defend systems, networks, software, hardware, and data from online threats is known as cyber security. It seeks to lessen the threat of cyber attacks and defend against the unauthorized exploitation of systems, networks, and technology. Cyber security is the safeguarding against cyber threats of internet-connected systems, including data, software, and hardware. To prevent unwanted access to data centers and other electronic systems, people and businesses utilize this technique.

A solid cyber security plan may give users and organizations a decent security posture against hostile assaults intended to gain access to, change, delete, destroy, or extort sensitive data and systems. A system's or device's activities being disabled or otherwise disrupted can be prevented with the help of cyber security.

The importance of cyber security

The need for cyber security is only going to expand as there are more people, devices, and software applications in today's businesses, along with an abundance of data—many of it sensitive or secret. the quantity and sophistication increasing of cyber attackers and attack methodologies exacerbate the issue.

- The subject of cyber security may be divided into a number of distinct parts, and it is essential for an organization's cooperation within that field to have a successful cyber security program. The following is a list of these sections:

- Application_security

- Information or data_security

- Network security

- Disaster_recovery/business_continuity_planning

- Operational_security

- Cloud security

- Critical infrastructure security

- Physical security

- End_user education

It may be difficult for any firm to maintain cyber security in a threat environment that is continuously changing. Traditional reactive strategies, in which resources were allocated for defending systems against the most significant known threats while less significant dangers went undefended, are no longer an effective method. An adaptable and more pro-active strategy is required to keep up with shifting security dangers. Advice is provided by a number of significant cyber security consulting groups. For instance, as part of a framework for risk assessment, the National Institute of Standards and Technology (NIST) suggests using real-time evaluations and continuous monitoring to protect against both known and unidentified risks.

Due to the frequent global headlines of massive breaches, cyber security has been increasingly prominent in recent years. In nearly all instances, it is caused by human mistake, which is accomplished by opening an attachment and downloading malware or disclosing private information to hackers. Knowing how to defend against cyber attacks may significantly lower the likelihood of a data leak.

What are the principal cyber security difficulties?

Hackers, data loss, privacy concerns, risk mitigation, and evolving cyber security tactics all pose ongoing threats to cyber security. It is not anticipated that cyber attacks will decline very soon. Additionally, the emergence of the internet of things (IoT) has added attack access points, which increases the need to safeguard networks and devices.

The dynamic nature of security hazards is one of the most challenging aspects of cyber security. New attack methods are produced as new technologies are created and as technology is applied in novel or distinct ways. It might be difficult to stay on top of these regular assaults' modifications and advancements while also upgrading procedures to defend against them. Concerns include ensuring that all cyber security components are updated on a regular basis to safeguard against potential vulnerabilities This can be especially challenging for smaller firms that lack people and in-house resources.

Furthermore, corporations can collect a large amount of prospective data about individuals who utilize one or more of their services. As more data is collected, the probability of a cybercriminal attempting to steal personally identifiable information (PII) increases. For example, a company that saves personally identifiable information on the cloud may be the target of a ransom ware assault.

Organizations should do all possible to avoid a cloud compromise. Employees may unintentionally introduce malware into the office on their computers or mobile devices, thus cyber security strategies should include end-user education. Regular security awareness training can assist employees in doing their part to keep their firm secure from cyber threats.

Another cyber security concern is a scarcity of skilled cyber security workers. As the volume of data generated and used by organizations expands, so does the demand for cyber security personnel to evaluate, manage, and respond to problems. (ISC)2 estimates a 3.1 million workforce gap between needed cyber security positions and security specialists.

CYBER SECURITY AND BUSINESSES

The greatest issue that businesses confront today is the global cyber revolution.

Traditional business paradigms are becoming obsolete as companies compete in the digital economy. eCommerce, mCommerce, Big Data, Predictive Analytics, Cloud, Blockchain, Robotic Process Automation, Intelligent Automation, Internet of Things, Social Media, and other new enterprises provide several advantages.

However, with every opportunity comes danger, and cyber enterprises are no exception. Cybersecurity has emerged as a critical factor in ensuring the long-term and secure growth of internet enterprises.

Why Is Cybersecurity Critical for Businesses?

As the globe becomes more digital, business industries throughout the world benefit from the extra benefits of the internet. To complete commercial processes, companies might use big data and analytical technologies. However, with the increased usage of the internet comes a significant security risk - cybercrime. As hackers become more proficient and employ technological means to enter sensitive networks, cyber attacks are becoming more widespread. Unfortunately, many of these crimes have a negative impact on millions of individuals, halting various large-scale activities and posing a threat to vast databases. Because cyber security measures are the only genuine remedy to cybercrime, they are critical for organizations.

Cyber security is a collection of practices that businesses and organizations may use to secure their computer systems and data from unauthorized persons. It is the answer to the ever-increasing threat posed by hackers, privacy violators, virus transmissions, and online scams. Businesses have numerous digital activities, and it has become critical for them to maintain cyber security against cybercrime. Here are a few of the many reasons why cyber security is critical for businesses.

Productivity rises.

Corporate companies seek talent from a variety of business-related professions in order to improve the productivity, efficiency, and success of their workplace. Human resource managers are also using training and development programs to help their employees become more adaptable. Managers may encourage their cybersecurity team members to enhance their skills and knowledge as dangers increase. To safeguard their company from these hazards, they can enroll in master's degree programs in cyber security online. Individuals may keep focused on the topic at hand while still managing their academics and improving their abilities through virtual schooling.

Cybersecurity is critical for organizations since it contributes to higher overall productivity. It will only be achievable if the company recruits the proper personnel. For example, there should be specialists who understand how to keep infections at bay Otherwise, if a hack affects production, organizations risk losing a considerable number of key business hours. In addition, it would waste employees' time and effort, resulting in inefficiency. As a result, business productivity depends on cyber security.

All-In-One Solution

The emergence of constantly changing technology and its use in business provides more benefits than drawbacks. Technology is still one of the most crucial components for successful businesses. As a result, enterprises demand cyber security as a one-stop solution to cyber attacks. As a result of technological advancements, computer devices are vulnerable to cyber attacks by unauthorized individuals and strangers. As a result, businesses must use strategic cyber security to keep their networks safe.

Unfortunately, organizations have access to up-to-date and powerful technology, which hackers take advantage of. They are developing new methods for automating attacks utilizing AI and machine learning, which may jeopardize the security of several systems at the same time. As a result, businesses must now hire professionals and incorporate cybersecurity precautions into their daily operations. Similarly, as a result of COVID-19, businesses are increasingly depending on cloud computing, particularly in the aftermath of prior lockdowns, and staff are working from home. It has put crucial data and information stored online in jeopardy. As a result, cybersecurity has grown in importance.

Consistency in Website Performance

Entrepreneurs recognize the need of adapting their company to the new environment. As a result, most businesses actively maintain their websites. An online presence allows them to retain consumers from all around the world and to reach them with a simple click. However, one of the growing risks of digital business is that your website may go offline if your system becomes infected. An infected hosting server will compel your website to go offline, leaving your online consumers susceptible to insecure networks. Customers will lose faith in you and your website, and your brand's reputation will suffer as a result.

It will also result in significant losses for your company because restarting the website might be costly, and the trust gap will result in the loss of multiple consumers. A website outage would also result in lost revenue due to missed transactions and a delay in replying to clients.

Cybersecurity can assist you in navigating such difficulties before they become too difficult to manage. It facilitates the secure networking of companies and customers. It will safeguard your system from long-term harm and viruses while also improving the seamless operation of internet operations.

It shields the company from losses.

Businesses and organizations must become more aware of cyberattacks and cybercrime. A cybersecurity system can assist organizations avoid cybercrime such as hacking, phishing, and fraud. For example, if a company's data is stolen, critical information might get into the wrong hands. It would result in exorbitant fines and stringent laws. As these hazards become more prevalent, the government has begun enacting new rules and regulations to safeguard consumers. It will hold the company liable for failing to take cybersecurity safeguards when dealing with consumers' personal information.

Furthermore, in the instance of hacking and theft, recovering the data, money, and time may be prohibitively expensive. It has the potential to produce massive deficits and losses for enterprises which might swiftly force a bankruptcy filing. These substantial financial losses might take years to recoup from and can only be averted by cybersecurity. Not only that, but these losses would harm the company's brand, which is especially important for publicly traded companies. We have multiple examples of large corporations that saw a dramatic drop in equity when stockholders sold their equities immediately after the systems were hacked.

Increases security

It would be foolish not to have access to consumer analytics and data in order to advertise your product effectively. However, maintaining sensitive information about the public puts the institution at danger of hacking. Fortunately, with the correct cyber protection, you can empower your organization on a digital platform while also providing a secure area for your employees, customers, and other stakeholders. They may believe in your company, invest in it, and purchase from it. Most significantly, cybersecurity would allow them to perform financial transactions with your company without worry.

FACTORS FOR AN EFFECTIVE CYBER SECURITY DEFENSE

When it comes to cybersecurity, there is no silver bullet answer. Every day, new vulnerabilities are identified, and IT professionals must always win the cybersecurity war, but attackers only need to win once to get a foothold in an environment. So, where should you concentrate your efforts to keep your business safe? This article will examine your cybersecurity defensive approach in depth.

Among cybersecurity professionals, defense in depth is a well-known concept. This technique employs many layers of security measures to secure the confidentiality, integrity, and availability of information systems. Your firm most likely already has numerous levels of security controls in place, but you may be wondering which ones are the most effective or give the most protection.
Let's look at the key elements of a cybersecurity defense in depth strategy.

The 5 Key Elements of a Cybersecurity Defense in Depth Strategy

Cybersecurity is a comprehensive concept that needs a number of components to be effective. Having stated that, these five components are essential for an efficient cybersecurity defense in depth approach.

PATCHING

The simplest way to reduce cybersecurity risk is to keep all of your systems, applications, and software dependencies up to date with the latest patches. Patch management is an essential component of any vulnerability management program, and with good reason. There are many of patch management software available, each with its own set of advantages and disadvantages. The main considerations here are that patches be implemented as soon as feasible, that all systems, applications, and third-party libraries are included, and that the program is audited on a regular basis to ensure objectives are fulfilled. TRAINING

Whether you realize it or not, your firm already has a fleet of security sensors deployed: your employees! These individuals are also your first lines of protection. Training is essential for both of these reasons. Users should be aware of potential risks like as phishing or social engineering, but they should also be educated to spot and report anything unusual or suspect. Users do not need to be trained to diagnose or triage situations, but they must know when to escalate to IT, who may then take the necessary measures.

SECTIONING AND MONITORING

"We can't analyze what we can't access," I frequently tell customers. This also applies to hackers and viruses. A system cannot be used if it is inaccessible. Unfortunately, improper network segmentation remains widespread. Network segmentation is the technique of dividing a logical network into zones and restricting data flow across those zones. By default, these zones should be set to block (or refuse) all traffic, with allow rules in place for protocols or services that enable critical business processes.

Effective network monitoring is made feasible by restricting data flow between network zones. Network monitoring cannot be successful if a network is not segregated and all ports and protocols are allowed. An attacker's ability to operate a protocol over a non-standard port, which could completely circumvent network monitoring efforts or Data Loss Prevention (DLP) controls.

LEAST PRIVILIGE PRINCIPLE

According to NIST, the Principle of Least Privilege states that "users and programs should only have the privileges necessary to complete their tasks." This is similar to the previous item, network segmentation, in that only necessary privileges should be authorized, just as only necessary data should be allowed to flow between network zones. Although this idea is highly reasonable, it is more easier stated than done, particularly in current setups where users' access rights or privileges must be removed.

Convenience far too frequently takes precedence over security. Removing users' local administrator capabilities and the use of separate accounts are two wonderful instances of when the concept of least privilege may not be comfortable but may be incredibly effective for privileged acts Both of these techniques improve security by preventing the installation of unwanted software, including malware, and by preventing users from disabling security features or changing system settings.

The Final Verdict

Effective cybersecurity involves layers, much like onions or ogres. The more layers of controls we can implement, the more obstacles an attacker must cross. Having these five important elements in place helps to create an effective cybersecurity defense in depth plan.

Do you have any doubts about the effectiveness of your security controls? LMG Security offers services to assist you in analyzing, testing, and enhancing your cybersecurity posture. Risk assessments, software patch management audits and upgrades, and cybersecurity training are all part of the service.

Privileged accounts, whether local or domain accounts, are popular targets for attackers because they may be used to move laterally, create persistence, manipulate logs, and even disseminate malware throughout a network, as is common in ransomware attacks.

HOW CYBER CRIMINALS STEAL CREDIT CARD INFORMATION

Cybercriminals have various tools at their disposal for hacking and exploiting credit card information. Learn about these, how to avoid them, and what to do if you are hacked. Cybercriminals have various tools at their disposal for hacking and exploiting credit card information. Learn about these, how to avoid them, and what to do if you are hacked.

Given the continuous growth of e-commerce and online transactions, cyber security has never been more important. Hackers may seek to compromise our privacy in a variety of ways, but one area that they find particularly appealing is credit card information. Stolen credit cards can harm not just your finances but also your personal identification and privacy. Effectively securing them and the data associated with them is critical in the online world. In this chapter, we look at how cybercriminals can steal your credit card information, highlight best practices to keep you safe, and explain what to do if your credit card is hacked.

Typical ways credit cards information are stolen

Hackers can steal credit and debit card information in a variety of ways, both online and offline.

1. Phishing

Can a website steal your credit card information? The short answer is yes.

Hackers use phishing to gain vital information by imitating a trustworthy source. Phone calls, bogus websites, and sales emails are all examples of phishing tactics.

For example, someone pretending to be from your issuing bank or credit card business phones and says they need to verify your credit card activity with some personal information and begins by asking for your credit card number. Alternatively, a phishing email posing as a merchant giving you a discount or free things could be sent to you attempting to dupe you into divulging account information

How to Avoid: The easiest approach to avoid phishing scams, whether by email, phone, or text, is to never provide personal or credit card information unless you started the contact. Also, conduct business directly on a retailer's website to ensure complete control over all transactions.

2. Spyware and malware

Take care with what you download.

Inadvertently downloading malware or spyware allows criminals to access information stored on your computer, including credit card information and other sensitive information. Malware may have a keylogger, which captures your keystrokes or browsing history and sends it to a hacker.

How to avoid:Avoid downloading attachments unless they come from a trusted source, and be cautious of the programs you download and install on any of your devices. Additionally, utilize antivirus software to detect malware before it affects your machine.

3. Sliding

Credit card skimming is a popular offline method used by criminals to collect personal information at a point of sale, which can also lead to identity theft.

Card readers at ATMs, petrol pumps, and other sites can be altered with to install skimming devices. These imposter readers collect and transmit payment information to fraudsters, who clone the cards and use them as they see fit.

Inspect outdoor credit card readers for indicators that they have been tampered with.

RFID skimming is a technique that uses radio frequency identification technology to wirelessly intercept RFID chip-based credit, debit, and ID information directly from cards or even smartphones and tablets. They use near-field communication devices to record unencrypted data from the card or a device's RFID chip in order to steal card details like numbers, expiration dates, and card holder names.

How to avoid: Check that your financial institution has adequate security measures in place, such as encryption

Shoulder surfing is a type of skimming that does not require any special equipment. A thief simply observes a user entering their ATM code or credit card information into a phone. This can be done close by (over the shoulder) or far away (via binoculars, for example).

 How to avoid: Protect keypads with paperwork, body, or clothing.

4. Wi-Fi networks in public places

Unsecured public Wi-Fi networks pose some risk if you connect to them and enter important information. While airport or hotel Wi-Fi might be handy, steps should be taken to prevent credit card and other important information from being lost. Furthermore, if "Free Public Wi-Fi" appears on your device, it might be a hacker on a nearby smartphone or laptop attempting to sign up unsuspecting people in order to steal your personal information.

Avoid conducting critical business when connected to public networks. If you need to connect to these networks, you should utilize a VPN. Otherwise, use your wireless cellular data connection or stick to trustworthy authenticated access points and Service Set Identifiers.

5.Your Trash

While it may appear archaic, criminals can dig through your garbage to find credit card statements, account information, and other valuable information.

How to Avoid: Select the option to receive credit card bills through email. If you do receive paper statements, destroy them once you've finished with them.

Best practices for credit card data security

Cybercriminals might obtain your credit card through a variety of techniques. Here are some suggestions to help you avoid this.

1. Examine credit reports

Credit monitoring and identity protection services like LifeLock keep track of your credit card activities. They can also assist you get ahead of any fraudulent behavior sooner than if you checked your statements manually.

2. Keep an eye on bank accounts and credit card statements for any unusual activity.

Manually reviewing credit statements and monitoring Equifax, Experian, and TransUnion for purchases you don't recall making might alert you to unusual transactions and questionable activity.

3. Configure alerts to warn you of any unusual activities.

Bank notifications through text, push notifications, and/or email can assist you in identifying suspicious transactions as soon as they occur.

4. Make use of antivirus software and VPNs.

When connecting to public networks, it's a good idea to use a VPN to protect yourself from viruses and hackers. Not to add that antivirus software can safeguard you if you inadvertently download malicious viruses.

5. Look for a secure URL on websites.

While visiting any website, but especially when making online purchases, be sure the URL has https:// and is secure.

6. Avoid storing credit card information on websites.

It might be tempting to save your credit card information on Google or at popular e-commerce sites. However, you should avoid this behavior since it might provide hackers access to your sensitive information. Text, push notifications, and/or email can assist you in identifying suspicious transactions as soon as they occur.

4. Make use of antivirus software and VPNs.

When connecting to public networks, it's a good idea to use a VPN to protect yourself from viruses and hackers. Not to add that antivirus software can safeguard you if you inadvertently download malicious viruses.

5. Look for a secure URL on websites.

While visiting any website, but especially when making online purchases, be sure the URL has https:// and is secure.

6. Avoid storing credit card information on websites.

It might be tempting to save your credit card information on Google or at popular e-commerce sites. However, you should avoid this behavior since it might provide hackers access to your sensitive information. in the event of a data breach

7. Make good use of secure passwords and two-factor authentication.

Another strategy to avoid being a victim of a data leak is to create strong passwords that include a combination of letters, numbers, and symbols. Two-factor authentication can provide an extra degree of protection to your account. Consider utilizing it when it is available.

8. Never write down your credit card details.

Finally, avoid writing your credit card number, PIN, expiration date, and other personal information everywhere or uploading images of your credit card number online.

 What should you do if your credit card information is stolen?

Following the best practices in this chapter will help keep your credit card information safe. However, nothing is foolproof. If your information is stolen, you may need to take action.

Here's what you should do.

1. Contact your credit card company

If you suspect your card has been stolen or compromised, the first thing you should do is call your bank or credit card company. This can help you avoid further damage and liability for fraudulent purchases. Your credit card company will cancel your card and issue you a new one.

2. Update your passwords

Hackers can employ a variety of online methods, including data breaches, malware, and public Wi-Fi networks to steal your credit card details and personal information Updating your passwords on any websites you frequent on a regular basis will help prevent them from having access to this information.

3. Examine and contest credit reports

Even if you deactivate your credit card, there may be certain transactions that you are unaware of. Continue to keep an eye on your credit statements so that you may challenge any questionable purchases.

Credit cards are a popular target for hackers, and this trend is unlikely to alter anytime soon. The first step in protecting yourself is to be aware of the ways they employ to acquire personal information, particularly credit card data, but also other facts that might lead to, among other things, identity theft.

23

Knowing the tactics they employ to steal credit card information,the first step in protecting yourself is to secure your personal information, in particular, but also other types of personal information that can lead to, among other things, identity theft. Implement the recommended measures outlined in this article to protect your credit information and take a more active part in avoiding being a victim of fraud.

ABOUT THE AUTHOR

Joel Pearson is a cyber security expert and a software developer who teaches businesses to take good cyber security measures.

25

27

29